Table of Conte

11. Maintaining Your Device
11.1. Tips for battery health and longevity.
11.2. Cleaning and caring for your iPhone.

12. Conclusion
* Recap of the highlights.
* Encouraging the exploration of iPhone features.

Disclaimer and Encouragement for Consulting Official Apple Resources

1. Introduction

1.1 Overview of the Latest iPhone Model

The latest iPhone model introduces a series of innovations that significantly enhance user experience. This device features a new, exceptionally efficient A15 processor, ensuring smoother app performance and more effective battery life. The camera has undergone a thorough redesign, now offering night mode in every lens, allowing for clear photos even in low light conditions. The latest iPhone model is also equipped with the latest version of the iOS operating system, bringing new, intuitive functionalities and improved security features.

1.2 Brief History and Evolution of the iPhone

The history of the iPhone is a fascinating journey through innovation and design. Since the introduction of the first iPhone in 2007, each subsequent model has brought groundbreaking changes, such as the introduction of the App Store, Touch ID and Face ID technologies, and continuous enhancements to the camera. The iPhone has transformed how people communicate, engage with media, and manage their daily lives.

Each new version is a testament to Apple's commitment to innovation and the pursuit of excellence, with the latest iPhone model being the latest example of this philosophy.

2. Getting Started

2.1 **Unboxing and Initial Setup**

Congratulations on your new iPhone! The moment you've been waiting for has arrived—unboxing your brand-new device. Here's how to get started:

1.Unboxing:
- Carefully open the box and remove the iPhone.
- You will find the iPhone, a USB-C to Lightning cable, and documentation.
- Please note that the power adapter and EarPods are not included in the box.
- Remove any protective film from the iPhone screen.

2. Powering On:
- Press and hold the side button until the Apple logo appears.
- You'll be greeted with "Hello" in different languages, signifying the start of the setup process.

3. Initial Setup:

- Follow the on-screen instructions to set up your iPhone. This includes language selection, connecting to Wi-Fi, and setting up Face ID or Touch ID.
- When prompted, you can transfer data from your previous iPhone or set up your new iPhone as a new device.
- Sign in with your Apple ID or create a new one if you don't have one. This is crucial for accessing Apple services like the App Store, iCloud, and more.
- Set up Siri, Apple's voice-controlled personal assistant, if you wish.

4. Final Steps:

- Once the initial setup is complete, you can start personalizing your device. This includes setting wallpapers, ringtones, and downloading your favorite apps from the App Store.

2.2 Understanding the Basic Interface and Gestures

The iPhone is renowned for its intuitive interface and fluid gestures. Here's a primer on navigating your iPhone:

1. Home Screen:

- The home screen is where you'll find all your apps. You can swipe left or right to view more apps.
- The dock at the bottom of the home screen can hold up to four apps or folders, and it's accessible from any of your home screen pages.

2. Control Center:

- Swipe down from the top-right corner of the screen to access the Control Center. Here, you can toggle airplane mode, Wi-Fi, Bluetooth, and other settings.

3. Notification Center:

- Swipe down from the top-left corner to access the Notification Center. Here, you can view all your recent notifications.

4. Gestures:

- **Swipe up from the bottom edge** (on iPhones without a Home button) or **press the Home button** (on models with a Home button) to return to the Home screen.
- **Swipe up and hold** to access the App Switcher, where you can switch between recently used apps.
- **Press and hold** on an app to access quick actions and contextual menus.

5. Taking Screenshots:

- Press the side button and the volume up button

simultaneously to take a screenshot.
- The screenshot preview will appear in the bottom left corner. Tap it to make edits or swipe left to dismiss it.

By familiarizing yourself with these basics, you'll be well on your way to mastering your new iPhone. In the following sections, we'll dive deeper into the rich features and functionalities your iPhone has to offer. Stay tuned!

3. Customization

Customizing your iPhone is a fantastic way to make the device truly yours. This section will guide you through personalizing your home screen and lock screen, as well as changing ringtones, alert tones, and system sounds to suit your preferences.

3.1 Personalizing Your Home Screen and Lock Screen

Your iPhone's home screen and lock screen are the first things you see when you use your device, so let's make them reflect your style and preferences.

1. Changing Wallpaper:

- Go to Settings > Wallpaper > Choose a New Wallpaper.
- You can select from dynamic, stills, or your own photos. Dynamic wallpapers move subtly.
- Once you've made your choice, you can set the wallpaper for your lock screen, home screen, or both.

2. Organizing Apps:

- Touch and hold any app on the home screen, then tap Edit Home Screen. The apps begin to jiggle.
- Drag apps to rearrange them. To create a folder, drag an app onto another app.
- Tap Done or press the Home button (on models with a Home button) when you finish.

3. Widgets:

- Widgets provide information at a glance and can be added to both your home screen and lock screen.
- Touch and hold a widget or an empty area in Today View until the apps jiggle, then tap the Add button in the upper-left corner.
- Select a widget, choose from three widget sizes, then tap Add Widget.

4. Lock Screen Customization (iOS 16 and later):

- Press and hold the lock screen to enter the customization mode.

- Tap the blue '+' button to create a new Lock Screen.
- Customize by adding widgets, changing the clock font and color, and setting a photo or dynamic wallpaper.

3.2 Changing Ringtones, Alert Tones, and System Sounds

Personalizing how your iPhone sounds can make your device feel even more unique. Here's how to change the ringtones and system sounds:

1. Changing Ringtones and Text Tones:
- Go to Settings > Sounds & Haptics.
- Under Sounds and Vibration Patterns, tap the sound that you want to change.
- Tap a ringtone or alert tone to listen to it and set it as the new sound.

2. Purchasing New Ringtones:
- Tap Tone Store to browse and buy new ringtones if you want something different.

3. Setting Up Emergency Alerts:
- Go to Settings > Notifications.
- Scroll to the bottom and under Government Alerts, toggle on the alerts you want to receive.

4. Adjusting Keyboard Clicks and Lock Sounds:
- Go to Settings > Sounds & Haptics.

- Scroll down to find the options for keyboard clicks and lock sound. Toggle them on or off according to your preference.

By taking these steps, you can ensure your iPhone represents your style and preferences, both visually and audibly. Enjoy making your device uniquely yours!

4. Communication Essentials

Effective communication is crucial, and your iPhone is a powerful tool that can keep you connected with the world. This section covers mastering calls, messages, and emails, and provides tips for using FaceTime and iMessage efficiently.

4.1 Mastering Calls, Messages, and Emails

Your iPhone makes communication seamless, whether it's through a phone call, text message, or email. Here's how to manage these effectively:

1. Managing Calls:
- **Making Calls:** Open the Phone app, choose a contact or dial a number, and tap the call button.

- **Receiving Calls:** Answer by swiping the green button or decline by swiping the red button. You can also send a quick message or set a reminder to call back later.
- **Blocking Numbers:** Go to Settings > Phone > Blocked Contacts to add numbers you wish not to receive calls from.

2. Using Messages:

- **Sending Texts:** Open the Messages app, tap the compose button, enter a contact or number, write your message, and tap send.
- **Adding Attachments:** Tap the camera icon to take a photo or video, or the photos icon to choose from your library.
- **Group Messaging:** Create group messages by adding multiple contacts in the recipient field.

3. Managing Emails:

- **Setting Up Email Accounts:** Go to Settings > Mail > Accounts > Add Account.
- **Composing Emails:** Open the Mail app, tap the compose button, enter the recipient's email, subject, and your message.
- **Organizing Emails:** Use mailboxes to categorize emails or swipe left on an email for more options like flagging or archiving.

4.2 **Tips for Effective Use of FaceTime and iMessage**

FaceTime and iMessage are powerful tools for video and audio calls, and text messaging respectively. Here are some tips to use them effectively:

1. FaceTime:
- **Making Calls:** Open the FaceTime app, enter the contact's name, phone number, or email address, and tap the video or audio icon.
- **During Calls:** Use features like flipping the camera, muting, or adding filters and Memojis.
- **Group FaceTime:** You can video call multiple people at once by adding more contacts during the call.

2. iMessage:
- **Activating iMessage:** Go to Settings > Messages and turn on iMessage.
- **Sending iMessages:** Messages sent as iMessages (blue bubbles) are free over Wi-Fi or cellular data.
- **Features:** Use features like Animoji, Memoji stickers, digital touch, and message effects to make conversations more interactive.

By mastering these communication essentials, you can ensure that you're using your iPhone to its fullest potential, keeping in touch with friends, family, and colleagues effortlessly and effectively.

5. Camera and Photography

Your iPhone is not just a phone; it's also a powerful camera capable of capturing stunning photos and videos. In this section, we'll explore the camera app and its various modes and share tips for taking professional-quality photos and videos.

5.1 Exploring the Camera App and Its Various Modes

The iPhone camera app comes packed with features and modes that cater to a variety of shooting scenarios, whether it's a picturesque landscape, a fast-moving sports event, or a beautifully plated dish.

1. Accessing the Camera:
- Quickly access the camera from the lock screen by swiping left, or from the Control Center.

2. Camera Modes:
- **Photo:** The standard mode for taking pictures. Use Portrait mode with advanced bokeh and Depth Control for professional-looking photos.
- **Video:** Record videos by simply swiping to the video mode. You can adjust settings like resolution and frame rate.

- Time-lapse & Slo-mo: Capture slow-motion videos or speed up time with these creative modes.
- Pano: Create panoramic images by slowly moving your camera from one side to another.

3. Live Photos:
- Capture moments with motion and sound. Press and hold a live photo to watch it.

4. HDR (High Dynamic Range):
- Use HDR to automatically balance the shadows and highlights in photos, ensuring detailed and vibrant images.

5.2 **Tips for Taking Professional-Quality Photos and Videos**

Taking great photos and videos isn't just about having a good camera; it's also about understanding some key principles and techniques:

1. Composition and Framing:
- Follow the rule of thirds by using the grid feature in the camera settings. Place your subject at the intersection points for a balanced composition.
- Pay attention to framing and try different perspectives for more interesting shots.

2. Focus and Exposure:
- Tap the screen where you want to focus. Swipe up or down to adjust the exposure (brightness).

- For portraits, use the Portrait mode and experiment with different lighting effects.

3. Steady Shots:
- Keep your hands steady or use a tripod, especially in low light conditions or when taking long-exposure shots.

4. Utilizing Natural Light:
- Whenever possible, use natural light. Early morning or late afternoon provides soft, diffused light.
- Avoid direct sunlight or use it creatively for silhouettes and backlit photos.

5. Editing and Enhancing:
- Use the built-in editing tools in the Photos app to adjust brightness, contrast, saturation, and more.
- Experiment with filters to give your photos a unique look.

6. Video Tips:
- For videos, keep your movements smooth and steady. Use features like time-lapse and slo-mo for creative effects.
- Pay attention to audio quality; avoid windy or noisy environments.

By mastering your iPhone's camera features and applying these photography and videography tips, you're well on your way to capturing professional-quality photos and videos. Happy shooting!

6. Productivity and Work

Your iPhone is a powerful tool not just for communication and entertainment, but also for productivity and organization. This section will guide you through effectively using the mail and calendar apps, as well as utilizing notes, reminders, and voice memos to enhance your productivity.

6.1 Setting Up and Using Mail and Calendar Apps

Staying on top of your emails and schedule is crucial for productivity. Here's how to make the most of the Mail and Calendar apps on your iPhone.

1. Setting Up Email Accounts:
- Go to Settings > Mail > Accounts > Add Account.
- Choose your email provider and sign in with your email address and password.
- Customize settings like fetch intervals and notifications according to your preference.

2. Using the Mail App:
- Organize your inbox with mailbox folders and filters.
- Swipe left or right on an email to quickly archive, delete, reply, or mark it.
- Use the search feature to quickly find specific emails.

3. Using the Calendar App:
- Add events by tapping the plus sign and filling in details like date, time, location, and attendees.
- View your schedule in different formats (day, week, month, or list).
- Set alerts for upcoming events to stay notified.

6.2 **Notes, Reminders, and Voice Memos for Increased Productivity**

For jotting down ideas, setting reminders for tasks, or recording voice notes, your iPhone has got you covered.

1. Using Notes:
- Create new notes, make checklists, or add photos and sketches.
- Organize notes into folders and use the search feature to quickly find specific notes.
- Share notes with others for collaboration.

2. Setting Up Reminders:
- Create a new reminder, add details like time or location-based notifications.
- Organize your reminders into lists to keep track of different projects or tasks.
- Use Siri to set reminders hands-free.

3. Recording Voice Memos:
- Use the Voice Memos app to record audio notes, lectures, meetings, orany sound.

- Edit your recordings by trimming the start or end.
- Share your voice memos via email, messages, or save them to your favorite cloud storage.

By integrating these tools into your daily routine, you can streamline your tasks, manage your time more efficiently, and increase your overall productivity. Whether it's staying on top of your emails, scheduling your week, jotting down sudden inspirations, or setting reminders for your to-dos, your iPhone is the ultimate companion for work and productivity.

7. Entertainment and Media

Your iPhone is not only a tool for productivity and communication but also a gateway to a vast world of entertainment and media. From streaming your favorite songs on Apple Music to catching up on popular shows with the TV app, your iPhone brings a world of enjoyment right to your fingertips.

7.1 Using Apple Music, Podcasts, and the TV App

Dive into the realms of music, podcasts, and television with these built-in apps designed for an unparalleled media experience.

1. Apple Music:

- **Getting Started:** Open the Music app to access a vast library of songs, curated playlists, and live radio.
- **Creating Playlists:** Craft your own playlists by adding your favorite tracks.
- **Discovering New Music:** Use the 'For You' section to find new music tailored to your taste based on your listening history.

2. Podcasts:

- **Browsing Podcasts:** Open the Podcasts app to find and subscribe to a wide range of podcasts across various genres.
- **Managing Episodes:** Keep track of your listening with options to automatically download new episodes and delete played ones.
- **Creating Playlists:** Organize your podcasts into playlists for a seamless listening experience.

3. TV App:

- **Accessing Content:** Open the TV app to watch your purchased or rented movies and TV shows.
- **Discovering Shows and Movies:** Explore the 'Watch Now' section to discover recommended content based on your viewing preferences.
- **Apple TV+ Subscription:** Consider subscribing to Apple TV+ to access original shows and movies exclusive to Apple.

7.2 **Exploring the App Store for Games and Other Applications**

Your iPhone comes with the App Store, a treasure trove of apps and games that cater to every interest and need.

1. Discovering New Apps:
- Browse the 'Today' tab to find featured apps and games, along with stories and tips from the App Store editors.
- Use the 'Games' tab to discover new and popular games.

2. Managing Downloads and Purchases:
- Use your Apple ID to purchase and download apps.
- Enable 'Ask to Buy' or 'Screen Time' for family sharing and parental controls.

3. Staying Updated:
- Keep your apps up to date by enabling automatic updates in Settings, ensuring you have the latest features and security enhancements.

By exploring these entertainment options, you can turn your iPhone into a multimedia powerhouse, ensuring that whether you're in the mood for music, podcasts, movies, TV shows, or games, you're always just a few taps away from what you love. Enjoy the rich world of media and entertainment that your iPhone offers, and make every moment enjoyable.

8. Health and Accessibility

Your iPhone is a powerful tool that can contribute significantly to managing your health and wellness, as well as ensuring accessibility for all users. This section explores how to make the most of the Health app for your wellness and fitness needs, and highlights the robust accessibility features that make the iPhone a device for everyone.

8.1 Utilizing the Health App for Wellness and Fitness

The Health app is a central repository for all your health and fitness data, offering a comprehensive view of your health, so you can make informed decisions about your lifestyle.

1. Setting Up the Health App:
- Open the Health app and tap your profile picture to set up your Medical ID for emergencies and fill in details like your birthdate, weight, and height.
- Connect apps and devices that you use for fitness and health to get all your data in one place.

2. Tracking Activity:

- Use your iPhone or connect your Apple Watch to track daily activities like your steps, distance walked or run, and flights climbed.
- Set daily fitness goals and monitor your progress throughout the day.

3. Monitoring Health Metrics:

- Track health metrics such as heart rate, sleep patterns, and nutritional intake.
- Record data like blood pressure and glucose levels either manually or by connecting smart health devices.

4. Creating a Health Dashboard:

- Customize your dashboard to display the most relevant health metrics for you.
- Use the Health app to visualize trends over time and understand how your habits influence your health goals.

8.2 Accessibility Features for an Inclusive Experience

The iPhone is designed with powerful accessibility features that accommodate all users, including those with vision, hearing, mobility, and learning disabilities.

1. Vision Accommodations:

- **VoiceOver:** A gesture-based screen reader that lets you enjoy using your iPhone even if you can't see the screen.
- **Magnifier:** Use your iPhone as a digital magnifying glass.
- **Display Accommodations:** Customize display settings with options like invert colors, color filters, and Reduce White Point.

2. Hearing Accommodations:

- **Live Listen:** Use your iPhone to amplify sound in noisy environments.
- **Visual Alerts:** Use LED flash or on-screen notifications for alerts.
- **Hearing Aid Compatibility:** Connect your hearing devices to your iPhone.

3. Mobility Accommodations:

- **AssistiveTouch:** Customize how you navigate your iPhone if you have difficulty touching the screen or pressing buttons.
- **Voice Control:** Control your iPhone with just your voice.
- **Switch Control:** Navigate your iPhone with minimal gestures.

4. Learning and Literacy:

- **Guided Access:** Help stay focused on a task by limiting access to a single app and controlling app features.
- **Speak Screen:** Have the content of the screen read to you.

By leveraging these health and accessibility features, your iPhone becomes not just a device, but a personal health companion and an inclusive tool that adapts to meet various needs, ensuring everyone can harness its full potential.

9. Security and Privacy

Your iPhone is designed with advanced security and privacy technologies to protect your information. This section will guide you through setting up Face ID or Touch ID for secure authentication and managing your privacy settings to have control over your personal information.

9.1 Setting Up Face ID or Touch ID

Face ID and Touch ID offer secure and convenient ways to unlock your iPhone, authenticate purchases, and sign in to apps.

1. Setting Up Face ID:
- Go to Settings > Face ID & Passcode. Enter your passcode, then tap 'Set Up Face ID'.
- Follow the on-screen instructions to scan your face. You'll need to move your head slowly to complete the circle.

- Once set up, you can use Face ID to unlock your iPhone, authenticate payments, and sign in to apps.

2. Setting Up Touch ID:

- Go to Settings > Touch ID & Passcode. Enter your passcode, then tap 'Add a Fingerprint'.
- Place your finger on the Home button repeatedly to capture all edges of your fingerprint.
- Once set up, you can use Touch ID to unlock your iPhone, make purchases, and sign in to apps.

3. Managing Additional Settings:

- In the Face ID & Passcode or Touch ID & Passcode settings, you can customize features like iPhone Unlock, Apple Pay, iTunes & App Store purchases, and more.

9.2 Understanding and Managing Privacy Settings

Your iPhone offers comprehensive privacy settings, giving you control over your data and how it's used.

1. Location Services:

- Go to Settings > Privacy > Location Services to manage which apps have access to your location information. You can grant access while using the app, always, or never.

2. App Permissions:

- Apps may request access to information like your photos, camera, microphone, contacts, and more. You can control these permissions individually for each app in Settings > Privacy.

3. Apple Advertising:

- Go to Settings > Privacy > Apple Advertising to manage your ad preferences. You can opt-out of personalized ads if you prefer not to receive ads targeted to your interests.

4. Analytics & Improvements:

- Choose whether to share device analytics with Apple to help improve products and services. Go to Settings > Privacy > Analytics & Improvements.

5. Tracking:

- Control whether apps are allowed to track your activity across other companies' apps and websites for advertising or data brokers. Go to Settings > Privacy > Tracking.

By properly setting up Face ID or Touch ID and managing your privacy settings, you can ensure that your personal information is protected and that you have full control over how it is accessed and used. Your iPhone is designed to give you peace of mind by securing your data and respecting your privacy.

10. Advanced Features and Tips

Your iPhone is packed with a variety of hidden features and shortcuts that can enhance your user experience and make daily tasks more efficient. Additionally, knowing how to troubleshoot common issues can save you time and frustration. This section will guide you through these advanced features and provide helpful tips for troubleshooting.

10.1 Exploring Hidden Features and Shortcuts

Unlock the full potential of your iPhone by exploring these lesser-known features and shortcuts:

1. Back Tap:
- Customize double or triple taps on the back of your iPhone to trigger actions like taking a screenshot, locking the screen, or launching an app. Go to Settings > Accessibility > Touch > Back Tap.

2. Text Replacement Shortcuts:
- Create shortcuts for commonly used phrases. Go to Settings > General > Keyboard > Text Replacement, tap the plus sign, and enter a phrase and its shortcut.

3. Custom Vibration Patterns:

- Create custom vibration patterns for contacts.
  Go to Contacts, select a contact, tap Edit, then
  tap Ringtone or Text Tone, and choose Vibration
  > Create New Vibration.

4. Quickly Redial Last Number:

- Tap the green call button in the Phone app to
  redial the last dialed number.

5. Use Siri Without Speaking:

- Type to Siri by going to Settings > Accessibility >
  Siri, then turn on Type to Siri. This is helpful in
  quiet environments or if you prefer typing.

10.2 Troubleshooting Common Issues

Even the best devices can encounter issues. Here are
some common iPhone problems and how to
troubleshoot them:

1. iPhone Not Charging:

- Check the lightning port for debris and clean it
  carefully.
- Try a different cable or charger to rule out cable
  issues.

2. Apps Crashing or Freezing:

- Close the app and reopen it.
- Update the app or your iOS to the latest version.
- Uninstall and reinstall the app if the issue
  persists.

3. Battery Draining Quickly:

- Check battery usage in Settings > Battery to see which apps are using the most power.
- Enable Low Power Mode in Settings > Battery.

4. Wi-Fi or Cellular Data Issues:

- Toggle Wi-Fi or Cellular Data off and on in the Control Center.
- Restart your iPhone or reset network settings (Settings > General > Reset > Reset Network Settings).

5. Touch Screen Unresponsive:

- Clean the screen with a soft, slightly damp, lint-free cloth.
- Remove screen protectors or cases that might be obstructing the screen.
- Restart your iPhone.

By exploring these advanced features and being equipped to troubleshoot common issues, you can enjoy a smoother and more personalized experience with your iPhone, ensuring that it works efficiently for your daily needs.

11. Maintaining Your Device

Proper maintenance of your iPhone is essential to ensure its longevity and optimal performance. This section provides tips for maintaining battery health and guidelines for cleaning and caring for your device.

11.1 Tips for Battery Health and Longevity

The battery is a crucial component of your iPhone, and taking care of it can prolong its life and maintain its performance.

1. Optimize Battery Settings:
- Use Low Power Mode to extend battery life when it's running low by going to Settings > Battery and toggling on Low Power Mode.
- Enable Optimized Battery Charging in Settings > Battery > Battery Health to slow down battery aging.

2. Monitor Battery Usage:
- Check which apps are consuming the most battery by going to Settings > Battery. Consider limiting background activity for apps that use a lot of power.

3. Maintain Ideal Temperature Ranges:
- Try to use your iPhone in temperatures between

- 0° and 35° C (32° to 95° F). Exposing your device to extremely low or high temperatures can damage the battery and affect its performance.

4. Regular Charging vs. Full Cycle Charging:
- Frequent, partial charges are better for lithium-ion batteries than full cycle (0-100%) charges. Avoid draining the battery completely before charging.

11.2 **Cleaning and Caring for Your iPhone**

Keeping your iPhone clean and well-cared-for not only keeps it looking new but also ensures its functionality.

1. Cleaning the Screen and Body:
- Use a soft, lint-free cloth to wipe your iPhone.
- Avoid getting moisture in openings and don't use cleaning products or compressed air.

2. Cleaning the Ports and Connectors:
- Gently remove any debris from the lightning port with a soft, dry, lint-free cloth.
- If necessary, use a soft-bristled brush to gently clean the speaker and microphone meshes.

3. Cleaning the Ports and Connectors:
- Gently remove any debris from the lightning port with a soft, dry, lint-free cloth.
- If necessary, use a soft-bristled brush to gently clean the speaker and microphone meshes.

- Ensure cases and screen protectors are free of debris before installation as particles can cause scratches.

4. Handling with Care:
- Avoid dropping your iPhone or subjecting it to other impacts.
- Keep your iPhone away from contact with liquids, which can damage or impair its functionality.

By following these maintenance tips, you can help ensure that your iPhone remains in top condition, offering optimal performance and a longer life span. Regularly checking your device and being mindful of its care can go a long way in preserving its functionality and appearance.

12. Conclusion

As we wrap up this guide to mastering your iPhone, it's clear that your device is much more than just a phone—it's a versatile tool that can enhance various aspects of your daily life. From making communication seamless and managing your schedule to capturing stunning photos and ensuring your data is secure, your iPhone is equipped to handle it all with ease and efficiency.

Recap of the Highlights:

- We started by setting up your iPhone, familiarizing you with the basic interface and gestures, ensuring you feel comfortable navigating your device.
- We delved into personalizing your iPhone, making it truly yours by customizing the home screen, lock screen, and sounds.
- We explored the comprehensive communication tools like calls, messages, emails, FaceTime, and iMessage, ensuring you stay connected with your world.
- We unleashed the potential of the Camera app, providing tips to elevate your photography and videography skills.
- We discussed maximizing productivity with tools like Mail, Calendar, Notes, Reminders, and Voice Memos.
- We navigated through the entertainment options, including Apple Music, Podcasts, the TV app, and the vast world of the App Store.
- We highlighted the importance of health and accessibility, ensuring your iPhone contributes positively to your wellness and is accessible to all.
- We delved into the critical aspects of security and privacy, ensuring you know how to protect your information and manage your data.
- We uncovered hidden features and shortcuts,

- making your daily interactions with your iPhone more efficient and enjoyable.
- Finally, we shared essential tips for maintaining your device, ensuring its longevity and optimal performance.

Encouraging the Exploration of iPhone Features:

Your journey with your iPhone is just beginning, and there's so much more to explore and discover. Each update and new model brings innovative features and improvements. I encourage you to continually explore and experiment with these features. The more you learn, the more you'll find your iPhone to be an indispensable part of your daily life.

Remember, the iPhone is designed to be intuitive and user-friendly, so don't hesitate to dive into settings, try out new features, and personalize your device to suit your lifestyle and preferences. Your iPhone is a powerful companion that can assist, entertain, and connect you in ways you might not have imagined.

Enjoy the journey of mastering your iPhone, and may it bring convenience, joy, and innovation to your everyday life. Here's to unlocking the full potential of your iPhone, one tap, swipe, and click at a time!

Disclaimer and Encouragement for Consulting Official Apple Resources

While every effort has been made to ensure the accuracy and reliability of the information presented in this eBook, technology is always evolving, and the functionalities of the iPhone may change over time. Therefore, the information provided is intended as a general guide and may not reflect the most current developments or features.

Disclaimer:

Consultation with Official Apple Resources:
For the most accurate and comprehensive information, it is strongly recommended that users consult official Apple resources. Apple provides extensive support and resources that are regularly updated to reflect the latest changes and features.

If you encounter significant issues or require specialized assistance, it is best to seek support directly from Apple or an authorized service provider.

Resources Include:
- Apple Support Website: https://support.apple.com
- Apple User Manuals: Accessible via the Apple Books app or the Apple Support website.
- Apple Support Community: https://discussions.apple.com where users can ask questions and share solutions.
- Apple Retail Stores: Visit for in-person support and workshops on how to use Apple products.

By consulting these official resources, you can ensure that you receive the most accurate, reliable, and up-to-date information and support available for your iPhone.

Remember, exploring and understanding your device is a continuous journey, and official Apple resources are there to guide you every step of the way. Enjoy the journey of discovering all that your iPhone has to offer!